Living Language and Dead Reckoning:

Navigating Oral and Written Traditions

Living Language and Dead Reckoning:

Navigating Oral and Written Traditions

THE 2005 GARNETT SEDGEWICK

MEMORIAL LECTURE

J. Edward Chamberlin

RONSDALE PRESS
VANCOUVER

LIVING LANGUAGE AND DEAD RECKONING
Copyright © 2006 J. Edward Chamberlin

Ronsdale Press
3350 West 21st Avenue
Vancouver, B.C., Canada
V6S 1G7

Set in Minion: 11 on 15
Typesetting: Julie Cochrane
Printing: Island Blue, Victoria, B.C.
Cover Design: Julie Cochrane
Cover Art: Katsusika Hokusai (1760–1849). *The Great Wave of Kanagawa.*
    From the series "36 Views of Fuji." Colour woodblock print.
Photo Credit: Art Resource, NY. Private Collection.

Ronsdale Press wishes to thank the Canada Council for the Arts, the Government of Canada through the Book Publishing Industry Development Program (BPIDP), and the Province of British Columbia through the British Columbia Arts Council for their support of its publishing program.

LIBRARY AND ARCHIVES CANADA CATALOGUING IN PUBLICATION

Chamberlin, J. Edward, 1943–
  Living language and dead reckoning : navigating oral and written traditions / J. Edward Chamberlin.

ISBN-13: 978-1-55380-037-8
ISBN-10: 1-55380-037-0

  1. Oral tradition — Commonwealth countries — History. 2. Commonwealth literature — History and criticism. I. Title.
PR9080.5.C44 2006   820.9'9171241   C2006-901227-X

INTRODUCTION

The first of the Sedgewick Lectures was given in 1955, six years after Dr. Sedgewick's death. Since then, distinguished speakers such as Hugh MacLennan, Northrop Frye, Robert Bringhurst, Sandra Djwa, William H. New, Michael Neill and most recently Angela Esterhammer have explored various topics from "Native American Oral Literatures and the Unity of the Humanities" to "Spontaneous Overflows and Revivifying Rays: Romanticism and the Discourse of Improvisation." Dr. Edward Chamberlin from the University of Toronto continues this fine series with his lecture on "Living Language and Dead Reckoning: Navigating Oral and Written Traditions."

The Sedgewick lectures are named in honour of Garnett G. Sedgewick, the first Head of the Department of English at the University of British Columbia, whose influence is still felt in the Department today. Dr. Sedgewick was hired by the University of British Columbia in 1918, and two years later became Head of the English Department, a post which he retained to 1948. He laid the foundations for the Department in the 1920's, nurtured it through the Depression years in the 1930's, and presided over its rapid expansion after World War II. Despite his many administrative duties he found time for scholarship as well. One of his areas of scholarly interest was Shakespeare, and his reputation was such that he was invited to give the Alexander Lectures at the University of Toronto in 1934. These lectures have subsequently been published under the title *Of Irony: Especially in Drama* and show a most learned man — we would call him "interdisciplinary" today — moving with ease from Old to Modern English, from German to Latin and to Greek.

By all accounts, Dr. Sedgewick was an outstanding teacher, a fabulous mentor to his students, and a man who deeply cared about the world around him, the latter being most evident in the semi-weekly column he wrote for the *Vancouver Sun* from September 1936 to October 1937, and which he ironically entitled "More Light than Heat."

This year's lecturer, Dr. Edward Chamberlin, a graduate from UBC, shares a thorough interdisciplinary background with Dr. Sedgewick. At present, Dr. Chamberlin is a Professor in both the English Department and the Centre for Comparative Literature at the University of Toronto. His interests, as is to be expected from someone in Comparative Literature, are manifold; they include modernist and contemporary poetry, West Indian literature, Aboriginal literature, oral and written traditions, and stories and story telling. His publications reflect these various interests. Dr. Chamberlin is the author of five books entitled *Horse: How the Horse Has Shaped Civilizations* (2006), *If This Is Your Land, Where Are Your Stories? Finding Common Ground* (2004), *Come Back to Me My Language: Poetry and the West Indies* (1993), *Ripe Was the Drowsy Hour: The Age of Oscar Wilde* (1977), and *The Harrowing of Eden: White Attitudes Towards Native Americans* (1975). In addition to these books he has published innumerable articles.

In this year's lecture Dr. Chamberlin explores the tension between oral presentations of tales and their written manifestations and poses the question: "What gets lost?" The teller, for one, his voice, and his inflection, but also the community of listeners. Reading is like "dead reckoning," a method of navigating on the sea in dense fog, in which one has no certainty except "that one is always almost lost." Reading is also like tracking in the sense that the track may convey the size of the animal, its speed, and the time it passed, but it will never be "the animal." In this portion of his lecture, Dr. Chamberlin inadvertently echoes Alfred the Great who looks at the books written by previous generations and comments in the Preface to his translation of Gregory's *Cura Pastoralis*: "Her mon mæg giet gesion hiora swæð" — "here one can still see their track," and ruefully continues "ac we him ne cunnon æfter spyrigean" —

"but we cannot follow their footsteps." Texts, it seems, useful as they are, also always remind us of the absence of the teller of the tale. This, unfortunately, is all too true of the text you hold in your hands.

— Gernot R. Wieland
Professor and Head

LIVING LANGUAGE AND DEAD RECKONING: NAVIGATING ORAL AND WRITTEN TRADITIONS

I'm sitting on the verandah at Halfmoon Bay, just north of Sechelt, looking out over Georgia Strait and the tugboats pulling log booms and barges down to the mills on the lower mainland. A purse seiner is heading towards Campbell River and the sheltered fishing grounds there, while in the distance over near Vancouver Island a trawler returns from a week at sea. They're at work, and all of them seem to know where they are going, and why.

There's an eagle soaring about, with menacing grace. His plans are a mystery to me, and maybe even to him, but his purpose is clear. Supper. Survival. He's at war with the world of ravens and rodents, and when he comes back to his nest high up in the fir tree he reminds me of George C. Scott playing General Patton.

A seal is doing flip-flops about twenty yards offshore. He arrives each morning about six, and returns every evening. I have heard that seals slap the water with their tails to stun the fish they've caught. He's doing no such thing. He's just playing around, showing off. I wonder what he does when we're not here.

Yesterday, as though to show him up, a school of dolphins went boiling by, leaping along on the way north to the fjords of the Inside Passage. They seemed absolutely sure of something. Either that, or they were out for exercise, like the fellow rowing to the lighthouse on Merry Island.

Watching all of this, I'm wondering about some old, old questions. Why do we work, and play, and wander about, and go to war? And why do we need stories and songs?

The fish and shellfish and the other sea life of the shore and shallow tidal pools go about their business, out of habit we might say. Habit, from the Latin *habitus.* In the Middle Ages, when you learned a language, it was said that you had the "habit" of it. We all live within our habits, and within our languages. That's part of the answer, I guess.

The other part is finding our way and feeding ourselves. Those are the two things we don't need an explanation for; they are aspects of human nature. Human beings are not the only creatures in this world that get lost and go hungry, but we make the most noise about it, going about the world looking for home, for something to satisfy body and soul, and then singing songs and telling tales about it. So nurture is involved too.

From ancient myths of lost and found to survival shows on TV, from physical exile to spiritual ecstasy, the theme is as old as humanity. So is the fascination with finding our way on the border between the world we know and the one we dream about, or dread. Somewhere in all this, literature and the arts come into their own.

In ecology, the edge or border is a place of both peril and possibility: the shore, for example, between the sea and the land where poets write so many of their poems; the borderland between the forest and savannah where humans and horses came into their own; the time between now and what's next. In Tlingit, there is a word that identifies the necessary conditions, material and spiritual, for storytelling. It's *shuka,* and like many important words, it's hard to translate. Nora Marks and Richard Dauenhauer, who have tried harder than anyone else to do so, suggest "before," meaning both ahead *and* behind — as in, "she walks before me" and "it happened the day before yesterday." Somewhere in that imaginative space — between here and nowhere, now and never — reading and listening happen.

*   *   *

*"Confrontation": a photograph by Adelaide de Menil taken
at Kingcome Inlet, British Columbia, 1968.*

11

Like all of us, I suspect, I've been lost many times. In cities, especially, but also in the country. I once got lost in the woods in upstate New York within hearing of a highway. And I've certainly been lost in the desert.

But I seldom feel lost in the mountains. Part of it has to do with familiarity, but even when I haven't been able to see the back of my hand, I can usually find my way. I think it has to do with mountains and rivers. The thing about mountains is, they go up; and rivers come down. It's simple. Find a river; and follow it. Go with the flow.

That's what we do in stories, of course; and it's why narrative is so comforting. It's hard to get lost in a good story, though some storytellers make us *feel* lost so that we can have the pleasure of getting found. Sometimes they even give us the illusion that we've found our selves. Most just set things up so that it all seems natural, like a river running down to the sea.

Mexican storytelling ballads, called *corridos,* even take their name from a word meaning "to flow," because that's exactly what they do. They roll along, like the Mississippi or the Columbia. It's not only the content that keeps them — and us — going; it's also the form. Rhythm comes from another river-like root, meaning motion; and so, not surprisingly, does emotion. The rhythm takes hold of us, and helps us find the way . . . by the feel of it, more than the thought. That's why the first act of good criticism is always irrational. Pleasure, after all, is an ancient test of truth and beauty and goodness.

Feeling is coming back into fashion in literary criticism, although these days it goes by the name of desire, and seems to be mostly about sex. Which is fine, because down deep, after the work and the play, the wandering and the warfare, it all has to do with the desire to live, to survive, to find ourselves in the world, to find a friend to keep us company. Feelings are central to this process; and so when we come across something that helps us find our way — a proverb, a poem, a prayer — we learn it by *heart.* The mind follows like a puppy in tow.

*   *   *

Let's go back to the sea, where it's easy to get lost and where the mind *has* to help us. Everything is moving there, usually in different directions: wind, current, tide, stars, the boat you're in. It's pure narrative, pure rhythm, pure verb. And what we want, as the waves wash over us, is a noun, a name, navigation.

On a good day, I might be able to find my way where the dolphins were heading, up Malaspina Strait past Jervis Inlet to Discovery Passage and the Johnstone and Queen Charlotte Straits. But not at night. Not when the fog rolls in. Not when I can't see, or hear very well. For that, I'd need the stories that have been told for centuries in coastal aboriginal communities, the ones that tell you exactly where you are. I once heard Yup'ik fishers in Alaska tell how when they were growing up they were taught to listen to such stories so carefully that if a fly landed on their nose they were not to brush it off, because if they lost their concentration and didn't get the words exactly right, in exactly the right order — order is everything in navigation — they would miss the harbour or offend the spirits or both. Or maybe I could make do with some of the new paraphernalia: a satellite signal, radar, GPS, one of those electronic methods.

Without either of these, if I wanted to find my way out there in the fog I'd need to know Dead Reckoning. It's not a cheerful phrase — some say it's a misspelling of the abbreviation "ded." for reckoning by deduction — but it's a method of navigation essentially unchanged since well before Columbus used it to navigate the Atlantic ocean and the Caribbean sea. The writer Robert Finley, who wrote a wonderful novel about Columbus called *The Accidental Indies,* tells (in an essay called "Reading as Dead Reckoning") how he learned dead reckoning from his father, with its "arcane formulas for triangulation and drift, for calculating speed through the water and speed over the ground, its tables, its protocols for record keeping, and its wonderful instruments of divination: the compass, the dividers, the parallel rules, the chart with its compass rose and its mysterious symbols, the taffrail log, the chronometer." All of this, in his words, help "to conjure up the harbour you've been hoping for." It sounds almost spiritual.

And indeed it does depend upon faith, and a set of ingenious figurations. Like the Tlingit *shuka*, it keeps you constantly on the edge, in this case between the real and the imagined.

The results of dead reckoning, Finley goes on to explain,

> come more in the form of a rhetorical than a mathematical position. The navigator sets out a position on a chart, but a good navigator always sets it out in pencil. In dead reckoning, as long as you can see and identify landmarks, you can fix a position, but as soon as you are out of sight of land, or the fog comes in, your sense of where you are depends on a single thread of narrative you spin as you go along. It is not for nothing that we say the navigator "plots" a course. . . .
>
> Good navigation relies on having good arguments for where you think you are, but a willingness to change your mind quickly . . . when things take a sudden and surprising turn [and] you are severed from a world you had understood to be out there. . . . All of the usual reference points become uncertain. . . . You imagined a bell-buoy, the opening of a known harbour, a white house on a hill. . . . Instead, [there is] a line of surf, a broken wall of cliff looming above you, or worst of all, sudden green water.

"There is something interesting that happens in the moment of sudden realization that things are not as you had thought them to be," Finley adds.

> In a way it is as though you had been posed a difficult riddle, a "who am I" riddle, where you yourself are the subject, and you find yourself entirely caught up in arriving at its solution. This moment can be at once terrifying and strangely liberating. Before a solution is found, this "riddle," for a giddy moment, opens the world to outlandish possibilities: since you are not where you thought you were, you might, for a moment, be anywhere at all.

Good navigation by dead reckoning is governed by the understanding that such moments as these are always possible, that one is always almost lost. It is, Finley concludes, like good reading, in which we learn to welcome those moments when we are both literally and figuratively at sea, lost in a book, overwhelmed by strangeness, carried along by the wind and the waves. "It is only half the truth to say that a book brings with it a world, discovers for us a new world. It also, necessarily, takes a world away, the world as we have habitually seen it. By doing so, it frees us, over and over, to a new recognition of where we suddenly are, of where we find ourselves to be."

*　*　*

Let me introduce another way of thinking about this by quoting Robert Bringhurst, in whose footsteps it is an honour to be walking in this year's Sedgewick Memorial Lecture. In *A Story Sharp as a Knife*, Bringhurst talks about reading as an ancient, preliterate craft:

> We read the tracks and scat of animals, the depth and lustre of their coats, the set of their ears and the gait of their limbs. We read the horns of sheep and the teeth of horses, the weights and measures of the wind, the flight of birds, the surface of the sea, snow, fossils, broken rocks, the growth of shrubs and trees — and of course we read the intonations of speaking voices. We read the speech of jays, ravens, hawks, frogs, owls, coyotes, wolves and, in infinite detail, the voices, faces, gestures, coughs and postures of other human beings. This kind of reading antedates all but the earliest, most involuntary form of writing, which is the leaving of prints and traces, the making of tracks.

I think he is absolutely right; but I also think he doesn't go far enough. Bringhurst celebrates a form of "reading" engaged in by those who are, in his words, "preliterate": in other words, by those who can't *really* read. I believe that they can, and do, and that we have much to learn from them about what it is to read.

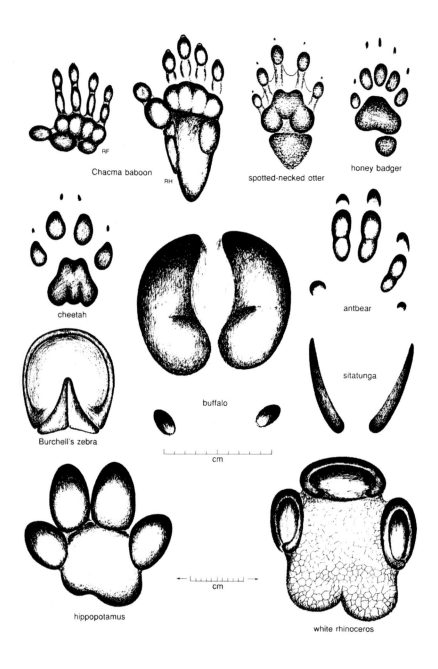

Chacma baboon

RF

RH

spotted-necked otter

honey badger

cheetah

antbear

Burchell's zebra

buffalo

sitatunga

cm

hippopotamus

cm

white rhinoceros

Tracks from animals in South Africa. Courtesy of Louis Liebenberg,
The Art of Tracking, *1990.*

But it's hard to get to that point, because even the best of us — and Bringhurst is among the very best — have a lot invested in a developmental model in which what we call literacy constitutes the major cultural achievement of European civilization, with the reading practices that emerged after the development of new print technologies signalling a change in human consciousness and new cognitive capabilities — specifically, a new awareness of the arbitrariness of signs, of the difference between a thing and the representation of a thing. (It is often argued that in due course this sponsored the new ways of reading the Book of Nature and the Book of God that became modern science and Protestantism.)

Many scholars seem convinced that it is only within the past few hundred years that this new consciousness came into being, and accordingly they identify written traditions with modern civilized societies and oral traditions with primitive peoples. "The eye analyzes, the ear tribalizes," proclaimed Marshall McLuhan, catching the wave. His student Walter Ong added to the catalogue, declaring (in his influential book *Orality and Literacy*) that oral cultures are imprisoned in the present, uninterested in definitions, unable to make analytic distinctions, incapable of separating knowledge itself from the process of knowing, and incorrigibly totalizing ("sight isolates, sound incorporates" is the catch phrase he uses, echoing McLuhan).

This is deceptively accurate — oral traditions, at least until new recording technologies, required us to keep company the way written traditions did not — but it is also demonstrable nonsense. And durable nonsense, unfortunately. Among other things, it creates the colonial and the postcolonial illusion that cultures are one or the other, oral or written. The fact is that there is no culture that does not involve both oral *and* written traditions. The major secular and sacred institutions of our supposedly "written cultures" — courts and churches and parliaments and schools — are arenas of highly formalized oral performance. And so-called "oral cultures" have a very wide range of written texts, from painted masks and beaded blankets to knotted strings and carved trays. These scripts aren't alphabetic, of course, but neither are the written forms of most of the world's languages.

And this nonsense not only separates people into primitive and civilized, it also interferes with our understanding of reading and listening. That is my interest here; not cultural ideologies in themselves (though it's hard to avoid them), nor the privileging of

Inca quipu: *coloured and knotted strings in which meaning is revealed by knot type and placement. Courtesy of E.H. Boone &* W.D. Mignolo, eds., Writing Without Words, *1994.*

thinking over feeling (which has such a hold on . . . well, on our *thinking*), but the ways in which we understand — and misunderstand — what reading and listening are all about.

To take reading first. The cognitive, cultural and behavioural advances that we associate with the development of reading practices in medieval and modern Europe were in fact flourishing thirty thousand years ago in the highly sophisticated reading practices of hunter-trackers around the world, who had an understanding of the contradictions of representation that is as complex as anything that we associate with the Renaissance.

The one thing trackers know when they see a track is that the animal isn't there. That's all they know. And they know that's all they know. In the stories that surround tracking in hunter-gatherer societies, both hunter and hunted are lost and each needs to find the other in order to find themselves. This knowledge is at the heart of hunting and tracking; and it is at the heart of reading.

Now I am not just talking about the ability of trackers to *see* animal signs. The systematic recognition of signs by traditional trackers is indeed remarkable, but it is not reading. Rather, it is a necessary preliminary, the way recognizing a script (like Arabic or Cyrillic) is. It's the first half of the process. The other half is interpreting the significance of the signs. Reading is qualitatively different from seeing; and it involves learning to recognize the difference between a thing and the representation of a thing — the difference between a bear and the word "bear," for example; or in the case of tracking, a bear and the sign or spoor of a bear. This is what tracking is all about, and it is what we do when we learn how to read. We learn that the word or the sign is the thing . . . which is to say, we learn that it is *not* the thing.

It's that riddle once again, that moment when we are between lost and found. We have gotten into the naive habit of giving most of the credit to ourselves for making our way, making sense, meeting the animal or the author. This shifts a bit with literary and philosophical texts, and even more so with religious texts where we are likely to acknowledge something of what Wordsworth called "peculiar grace, a leading from above, a something given." But we still see interpretation as *our* achievement, our discovery, maybe even our invention.

Ceci n'est pas une pipe *by René Magritte, inviting us to contemplate the difference between a pipe and the representation of a pipe.*

And yet we know that this is only superficially so, and that it is never easy to decide whether meaning and value are part of nature — part of the text, that is — or part of us. The philosopher Herbert Simon tells about watching an ant work its way along a beach. The surface is uneven, and the ingenuity of the ant in navigating across it is wonderful to behold. Except that the wonder, Simon suggests, might just as properly be in the beach rather than the ant. Looked at that way, it is the beach that is complex; the ant is just an ant, barely sophisticated enough to use the beach to find its way.

None of us would dismiss this line of logic in a good work of literature. We still celebrate the ways in which a text takes us in, and leads us along. We know that we have to be alert as well as humble for this to happen, like that good navigator Rob Finley talked about, always ready to be lost, so that when we realize that we're in the unfamiliar and the unknown we can — with either "practised calm or with heart pounding and the chart flapping in our hands" — begin the imaginative negotiation and the navigation necessary to find our way again.

This state of uncertainty — we sometimes call it indeterminacy or incompleteness — has a lot to do with language itself, and with

Carved wooden coastal charts carried in their kayaks by Greenland Inuit.
Courtesy of David Turnbull, Science is an Atlas, *1989.*

what is sometimes called linguistic relativity. It's a fancy name for a fairly simple, and very old, idea: that we experience the world — that is, we think and feel — in language; and that those who speak different languages therefore think and feel differently. According to habit. Behind this is the question of whether — and to what extent — language creates thought, or conveys it. In the past hundred years, this has been a matter of much debate, coinciding with debates about the interdependence of the observer and the observed. Linguistic relativists like Edward Sapir and Benjamin Lee Whorf argued for the determinism of language, while universalists like Max Black and Noam Chomsky insisted that we are all similarly coded for language. It is an issue over which intelligent people have disagreed for a long time. The argument had an earlier run in the late eighteenth and early nineteenth centuries, when Wordsworth and Coleridge took opposite sides. Wordsworth believed that language embodies thought (language is its incarnation was his image), while Coleridge was convinced that language communicates it (as a slide-rule — his analogy — calculates sums).

And what about feelings? Many argue that they are just as intimately determined by language, while others take a more instrumental approach. The difference of opinion finds its way into educational and political ideologies, with one side convinced that it is possible to change human nature by changing (or "correcting") language (including laws), and the other convinced that all one can do is control the way people think and feel and behave. But at the end of the day, whether we are relativists or universalists, thought and feeling remain dancing partners, like fate and free will, and language is the music.

One of the oldest questions about the origins of humanity is which came first, music or language. The ethnomusicologist John Blacking argued that "early human species were able to dance and sing several hundred thousand years before homo sapiens emerged with the capacity for speech as we know it," while Susanne Langer suggested that the festive dance and the creation of visual imagery supplied the conditions for language, with reading gestures possibly as important as listening to sounds. In any case, it was not words but *phrases* — musical phrases or accretions of sounds—that were the origin of language, in her opinion. This meant that from the beginning listening depended on recognizing a pattern, like the pattern of music, which effectively put reading and listening together as another set of dancing partners.

*   *   *

We need a history of listening comparable to our histories of reading. I don't mean a political or cultural history, valuable as those would be, but a history of the cognitive and affective dynamics of listening, its navigational principles. Surprisingly, there is very little scholarship along those lines. What we do have are some good discussions of performance, including a lot of studies of what are called performativity and theatricality; and some interesting work on the contradictions of belief in oral performance, which is where the ubiquitous figure of the trickster comes into his (or her) own. As the great Canadian storyteller Alice Kane used to recite:

The dreamer awakes
The shadow goes by
The cock never crew
The tale is a lie.

But harken it well
Fair maiden, good youth,
The tale is a lie
But the telling is truth.

Do we believe the teller or the tale? It's the oldest question in the study of oral traditions; and as with all riddles, we make a fundamental mistake if we think we have to make a choice between the truth of one or the other. It's a choice between form and content, or the real and the imagined; it's a choice between being marooned on an island and drowning in the sea. Nobody should make that choice. Ultimately, nobody can.

In the 1920s at the Sorbonne in Paris, while the Swiss linguist de Saussure was distinguishing between language as a system and language as a speech act, a quite different approach was being developed by Marcel Jousse. He argued that a sophisticated form of listening developed very early in human society with the recognition of something that he called "oral style," as distinctive as any written style and more or less common across cultures and through time. It is *not* exactly a style of speaking, according to Jousse, but a form of expression in which the physical presence of the performer is crucial, and where gesture and movement are fundamental; and it depends upon memorization. This style, while it underlines the difference between the teller and the tale, makes it absolutely impossible to distinguish between them. That's a start.

Although Jousse traced his interest in this back to his peasant roots in rural France and to his interest in Biblical traditions of performance, he did not believe that oral style was either ancient or primitive. On the contrary, it was something we all share ... *if* we don't destroy it in the benighted forms of education that he railed

Prophets listening to the Word (Book of Kells)

against, where children are told to sit down and shut up as a condition — a necessary and sufficient condition — of learning to listen. There goes movement and gesture; and memorization is unnecessary if we can just write it all down. Children, fortunately, know better; they save memorization for their *own* stories and songs.

Whether we know his name or not — his impact was enormous at the time, but time passes — we do understand what Jousse was on about, for we give a special place in our society to those adept at listening and finding meaning and value beyond the mere words: judges, doctors, therapists, teachers, priests, mothers, grandfathers, and friends. Many of the most important ceremonies in our society, secular and sacred, involve professional listeners, people who are paid to listen and by listening to give a particular kind of credibility to what is said.

This kind of listening does not come naturally. *Hearing* comes naturally, just as seeing does. But listening is like reading. We learn how to do it, just as we learn how to distinguish music from noise;

and we also learn that this distinction is, like writing scripts, culturally specific. But the process is universal. And so is the difference between listening for the letter and listening for the spirit. It's something like the difference between the teller and the tale. We attend to both, of course; but it is important to recognize in what order.

The distinction between letter and spirit has a long history in the study of reading, of course. Many scholars — my colleague Brian Stock among them — have pointed out that along with modern reading practices came a shift in priority to the letter rather than the spirit of a text. The spirit — the Holy Spirit in the Bible was the obvious reference — would be available through an interpretation of the letter, rather than by the literary equivalent of a lightning strike. It was mediation rather than possession, with the written text as mediator. This privileged the authority of the writer; and it created renewed interest in the relationship between the word and the intention behind the word (which is precisely what happens with signs in traditional tracking).

We can see this played out in Wallace Stevens' great poem "Ideas of Order at Key West," where the relationship between letter and spirit shuttles between singer and song, as well as between reading and listening. "She sang beyond the genius of the sea," the poem begins, describing a woman singing a song by the seashore:

> The song and water were not medleyed sound
> Even if what she sang was what she heard,
> Since what she sang was uttered word by word.
> It may be that in all her phrases stirred
> The grinding water and the gasping wind;
> But it was she and not the sea we heard.

> For she was the maker of the song she sang.
> The ever-hooded, tragic-gestured sea
> Was merely a place by which she walked to sing.
> Whose spirit is this? we said, because we knew
> It was the spirit that we sought and knew
> That we should ask this often as she sang.

Stevens accords his singer extraordinary power over the world of which she sings:

> It was her voice that made
> The sky acutest at its vanishing.
> She measured to the hour its solitude.
> She was the single artificer of the world
> In which she sang.

But ultimately there is something more, something that has to do with that spirit we are looking to find:

> Ramon Fernandez, tell me, if you know,
> Why, when the singing ended and we turned
> Toward the town, tell why the glassy lights,
> The lights in the fishing boats at anchor there,
> As the night descended, tilting in the air,
> Mastered the night and portioned out the sea,
> Fixing emblazoned zones and fiery poles,
> Arranging, deepening, enchanting night.
>
> Oh! Blessed rage for order, pale Ramon,
> The maker's rage to order words of the sea,
> Words of the fragrant portals, dimly-starred,
> And of ourselves and of our origins,
> In ghostlier demarcations, keener sounds.

I am well aware of how hazardous it can be to use a poet's words to pursue a critical argument. I began my career doing that, with Wallace Stevens in fact, and made every mistake in the book. But there is something suggestive here: the uncertainty of origins, represented by the sea; and the security of orderings, in the harbour. In between, there is a sceptical mind and a spellbound listener, wondering about means and ends, and seeking a sense of the spirit — word by word, you'll recall — which will give form and significance to the occasion, telling us who we are and where we belong.

*|Abakas Koper and |Una Rooi telling a story together at a rest stop
in the Kalahari Gemsbok (now the Kgalagati) National Park on their
first return to their ancestral homeland in forty years.
Photo courtesy of J. Edward Chamberlin.*

I'll come back to this spirit in a moment, but first to what
Stevens calls this "blessed rage to order," which portioned out the
seas, fixing zones and poles, arranging — as well as enchanting — the
night.

It is an old question whether the urge to order is primary; or
the urge to chaos. We seem to take almost primitive delight in dis-
order and derangement: witness the pleasure provided by the sig-
nature opening lines of poems — "I saw eternity the other night"
(Henry Vaughan); or "I have been seeing dragons again" (Michael
Ondaatje); or "I heard a fly buzz when I died" (Emily Dickinson);
and by the set-up of stories — "it was and it was not" (the traditional opening of Majorcan storytellers); or "once upon a time"; or
|garube, the word used by the Khoikhoi herders of southern Namibia
which means "the happening that is not happening." The ease with
which we surrender to melodies and rhythms is part of this too . . .

which is why almost every colonial jurisdiction in the late nineteenth century banned drumming and dancing. Music might just undo the empire, just as it will untune the sky. Certainly it still upsets a lot of households, to a chorus of "turn off that goddamn music!"

Of course, we could turn this around and say that we accommodate such confusion to bring our instinct for order into play. At the beginning of the twentieth century, the German art critic Wilhelm Worringer proposed what he called a "psychology of style" in which human responses were divided into two categories: empathy (which was a translation of the German *Einfühlung,* or feeling-into) and abstraction. Abstract forms, he argued, organize our experience of the world by giving us a sense of distance from it. Organic forms, on the other hand, invite us to surrender to their energies.

Worringer used this to develop a typology of art, but the fact is that most of us delight in — and depend upon — *both* abstraction *and* empathy, just as we do upon both clarity and mystery. Does this differ, does the centre of gravity shift, from reading to listening? Does one or the other leave us more lost than found, more famished than fulfilled? What difference does it really make whether we listen to a story or read it? Is one like going down a river, and the other like dead reckoning? Whatever the case, both require some surrender of sorts; and maybe the distinction is more like that between pressure on the rudder and wind in the sails.

*   *   *

A few years ago, I attended celebrations at two universities. One was the University of the West Indies. It was fifty years old, and for reasons of necessity — it serves fourteen different national communities, all of them islands — it has been at the forefront of developments in distance education. I admired its aspirations and achievements, but I was sceptical of its practices. Teaching at a distance seemed to me sort of like phone sex. A sleight of hand. Not the real thing.

Then I went to Charles University in Prague, which was founded in 1348. For six hundred and fifty years, during which Europe had changed almost beyond recognition, Charles University held on. In its early years, the university had a very large enrolment; up to twenty-five thousand students would come from across the continent to Prague to listen to the scholars gathered there, and to read the manuscripts that were in the library. Within a century or so, enrolment plunged tenfold. Why? Because of books. People didn't need to travel vast distances. They could read the words of their teachers from miles away. It was the beginning of distance education.

Now what was lost, other than a lot of students? Perhaps something to do with that spirit Stevens talked about, which makes music even more important than language in holding people together — young people, or political groups, or rugby teams. The deep comfort of being in company with others in an audience, and with the singer of the song or the teller of the tale, is important here. It's one explanation for the remarkable popularity of public readings. But more than that, it seems to give us nourishment, and a sense of direction.

What is it about this that generates such aesthetic enjoyment, as well such strong feelings of solidarity, at a rock concert, for example, or a service in a church or synagogue or mosque or sweetgrass ceremony. Whatever our answer, why would we settle for secondhand? And yet, more and more, we do.

I think of a story told by my grandfather, about the winter of 1886 on the prairies in southern Alberta. The snow wasn't so bad: the cattle could scrape and snuffle their way through to the grass below, though water was hard to find. But it was very, very cold, and they were having a tough time of it.

Then came a Chinook, a surprisingly warm wind that is quite common in the foothills of the Rockies. Chinooks work like a refrigerator in reverse. When westerly winds carrying moist air from the Pacific hit the mountains, the air cools as its rises, dropping rain and then snow. If the conditions are right, the now dry air will slide right down the eastern slopes of the Rockies ten thousand feet to the plains below. Cold air heats up when it falls, because the air is denser and the pressure higher at lower altitudes; and dry air warms twice as fast as moist air. The warm air pushing out the cold creates the wind called a Chinook, signalled by a wonderful arch of cloud in the western sky. It can raise the temperature dramatically, and melt an inch of ice an hour. Folks used to tell a story about a traveller who tied his team to a post sticking up in the snow one night. A Chinook came, and in the morning his horses were dangling from the church steeple.

My grandfather was on his way to visit a friend at Stand-Off, about fifty miles south of Fort Macleod, where he was living; but riding across the Oldman River, he saw the unmistakable Chinook arch, and small splashes of water. A Chinook was on the way. It was always welcome in the middle of winter, but it was also a warning. If the Chinook melted the ice, he'd be stranded on the other side of the river for days, maybe weeks. He turned around. He'd have to visit later in the spring.

The cattle and the horses also sensed a change, a new lease on life. They wouldn't have to scuffle and scrape any more. They looked up to the sky in a moment of faith, and stumbled on through the crud and the crust in a mellow mood. The temperature, which had been well below freezing that morning, was into the sixties by now. The snow started to melt; and before long they could see the grass underneath the water that covered the land.

But this Chinook was short lived. The cold weather came again, hard and fast, and within a few days the water was frozen so hard that the cattle couldn't break through. It was much worse now than it had been with the snow cover. All the cattle could do was look at the grass a few inches below the surface of the ice.

My grandfather made it; but thousands of cattle didn't. They starved to death that winter within sight of the food and water that would have kept them alive. It was as though all they had was food under glass. Or photographs of food.

Chinooks weren't new in my grandfather's time, but photographs were. Soon, the telephone, the radio, film, television, the wonders of vinyl, tape and disk recording, and then computers created a *virtual* world of sight and sound and motion. What kind of nourishment did all this provide? I've talked elsewhere about stories and songs as a covenant of wonder with the world. I sometimes think that the new electronic ways in which we can now listen leave us like those cattle, with a cruel promise, a broken covenant. And yet I'm not sure. Did books do that too?

Put differently, did something radically new begin around my grandfather's time with regard to traditions of oral performance and the communal experiences they generated; and if it did, was it comparable to the novelties of print technology and the new reading

A Mexican scribe (tlacuilo) and his son busy transcribing their people's history in the late sixteenth century at the time of the Spanish invasion. Courtesy of Codex Mendoza, Bodleian Library, Oxford.

practices they encouraged? Is there a renegotiation taking place right now between speaking and listening, between presence and absence, between the actual and the virtual? Or are we all going hungry?

Many of us now do most of our listening at a distance. What exactly are we missing, and how important is it? What have we gained, apart from not having to go all the way to Prague? When we listen to the radio or a recording, are we hearing someone speak, or overhearing them? Is a recorded voice like a translation from one language to another; and if so, what's lost in the translation? Is whatever is lost replaced by something else? Is the language of recording perhaps neither writing nor speaking, but something else, something new? What do we miss when we don't have the gestures, not to mention the other sights and sounds and smells, of the performance . . . the gooood grease, as the Tlingit say. And what do we miss when we don't have *company*?

Something, surely. It may vary across cultures, but I doubt it. In arguing for the place of oral performance in the traditions of literature, the South African literary historian Michael Chapman suggests that we have a choice between what he calls the hermeneutics of doubt and suspicion, and the humanism of belief and reconciliation. The latter, for him, is only available in congregation, which is why the Truth and Reconciliation Commission was so important.

And yet something powerful does take place as we listen to recordings, or the radio, some shift in the way we nourish ourselves and navigate this world, some change in the relationship between reality and the imagination, some new sense of community. Aristotle said that memory and imagination are located in the same part of the soul, because they both allow us to see and hear something that is not present. Perhaps a new kind of memory is taking hold, and shaping a new kind of imagining.

In any case, I am convinced that we should consider a major change in the way in which we think about oral performance. Listening to radio and recordings removes the uncertainties and indeterminisms that accompany live performance. It gives us a sense of confidence in where we are, like GPS. We no longer have to worry about whether we believe the teller or the tale. There is *only* the tale . . . and the *telling* is now the lie. If writing turns speech back on itself, making us aware of the presence of certain structural aspects of language and the absence of gestures and tones of voice (as David

Olsen has argued in his book *The World on Paper*), does recorded speech do something of this too, so that its affective losses become cognitive gains?

∗   ∗   ∗

In !Xhosa praise singing, the *imbongi* — especially when he is performing impromptu — often ends with a ritual phrase, "I disappear." In the new oral tradition which recording has ushered in, the performer says that when she *begins*. As we begin listening, the teller has disappeared, just like the author of a book. But unlike the author, he or she is still right there.

This is the new consolation, and the new contradiction. And it reverses the relationship between letter and spirit introduced by reading practices, whether neolithic or neoclassical. We need the letter — that's how we find our way, after all — but now we can only get at it *through* the spirit, rather than the other way around. There is no letter, except in our imagination. And the question of whose spirit this is comes back into the centre of such listening. In radio and recordings, it's a question that is impossible to avoid. That has got to be a good thing.

In 1908, Wassily Kandinsky promoted the new non-representational or "abstract" art in an essay called *Über das Geistige in der Kunst* — "Concerning the Spiritual in Art." He and his counterparts in the arts changed the way we saw and heard the world, and our expectations about art. "Whose spirit is this?" became the question everybody began to ask as they tried to understand how voices could come out of black boxes and people come to life on a silver screen.

Then Virginia Woolf, on her way to a lighthouse much like the one on Merry Island, said that "on or about December, 1910, human character changed." She was referring to the post-Impressionist exhibition at the Grafton Gallery in London, which ran from November 8 to January 15 and introduced new forms of representation in painting. But somewhere in her soul she must also have been conscious of the other changes that were altering the way people thought about what they heard and saw, and felt about listening and reading. I think she was right.

ABOUT THE AUTHOR

J. Edward Chamberlin was born in Vancouver, and educated at the universities of British Columbia, Oxford and Toronto. Since 1970, he has been on the faculty of the University of Toronto, where he is now University Professor of English and Comparative Literature. He has been Senior Research Associate with the Royal Commission on Aboriginal Peoples in Canada and Poetry Editor of *Saturday Night*, and has worked extensively on native land claims in Canada, the United States, Africa and Australia. His books include *The Harrowing of Eden: White Attitudes Towards Native Americans* (1975), *Ripe Was the Drowsy Hour: The Age of Oscar Wilde* (1977), *Come Back to Me My Language: Poetry and the West Indies* (1993), and *If This Is Your Land, Where Are Your Stories? Finding Common Ground* (2003). His latest book, *Horse: How the Horse Has Shaped Civilizations,* will be published by Knopf in 2006.